Pangbourne

AN ILLUSTRATED HISTORY

Pangbourne Reach from the tow path, c. 1900

Pangbourne

AN ILLUSTRATED HISTORY

Joan Wilcox

BERKSHIRE BOOKS

First published in the United Kingdom in 1992
by Berkshire Books

Copyright © Joan Wilcox 1992

British Library Cataloguing in Publication Data

Wilcox, Joan
Pangbourne: Illustrated History
I. Title
942.29

ISBN 0–7509–0225–6

BERKSHIRE BOOKS

Official Imprint of Berkshire County Council
Managed by
Alan Sutton Publishing Ltd
Phoenix Mill · Far Thrupp · Stroud
Gloucestershire

Typeset in 12/13 Sabon.
Typesetting and origination by
Alan Sutton Publishing Limited.
Printed in Great Britain by
The Bath Press, Bath, Avon.

Contents

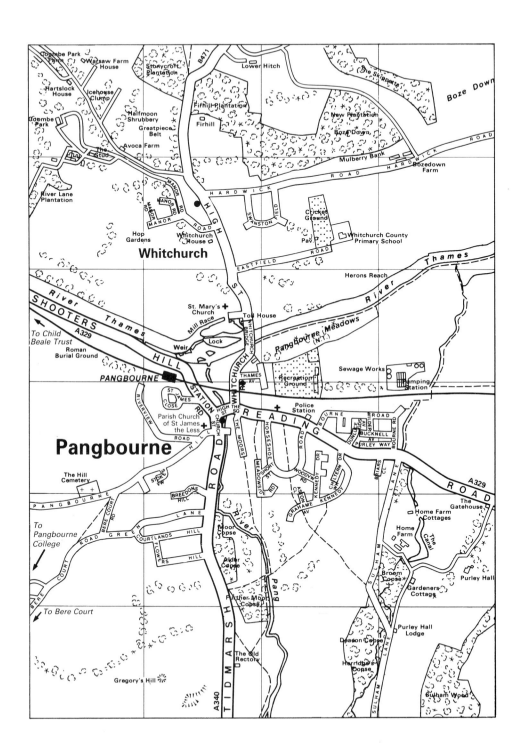

Acknowledgements

In compiling this book about Pangbourne I have been most grateful for the help I have received from many people in the village. I am particularly grateful to Mr Percy Stone, the grandson of Robert Stone, miller of Pangbourne, for his unfailing interest and consideration. The wealth of information from his grandfather's diaries, press cuttings of the 1890s and his own remarkable memory has been a valuable contribution to the book.

Many thanks also to Mrs Ruth Capildeo for her line drawings, Mrs Beryl Cox for memories of her school-days, Mr Peter Collier for his encouragement and Mrs Gaye Sumner, librarian at Pangbourne Library, for starting the ball rolling.

Finally, a word of appreciation to my husband for his tolerance in acting as back-room boy.

Joan Wilcox
1992

Picture Credits

The author and publishers would like to thank the following who have kindly loaned the material for the illustrations in this book:

Peter Woodage, Iris Moon, Percy Stone, Joyce Mornement, Berkshire Library Service, the Centre for Oxfordshire Studies, Oxford and the Child-Beale Wildlife Trust.

— 1 —

Early Beginnings

Pangbourne is first mentioned in a Saxon charter of 844 recording a grant of land by Ceolred, Bishop of Leicester to Burtulf King of Mercia.

> I, Bishop Ceolred, with the knowledge and permission of my venerable communities will give to Burtulf King of the Mercians, the territory of 14 hides at Paegingaburnam by the river which is called the Thames in return for the liberty of these monasteries that he may have, enjoy and possess the same land for his life and leave it to whomsoever he shall wish after him in perpetual inheritance . . .

Paegingaburnam, the ancient name for Pangbourne, means 'the stream of the sons of Paega' which could be the name of the leader of a Saxon group who had settled here.

Although there is no precise record of a Roman settlement in Pangbourne, Roman coins, urns and a possible Roman cemetery were excavated when the railway was being constructed through the parish. Traces of a Roman villa were discovered nearby when the M4 motorway was being built.

Pangbourne formed part of the diocese of Wessex after St Birinus, known as the Apostle of the West Saxons, baptised King Cynegils in AD 635 and established his See in Dorchester on Thames. Before the Norman Conquest Pangbourne was divided into two portions. The smaller of these, assessed at two hides, was said in the Domesday survey to have 'belonged to the ferm' (farm) in the reign of Edward the Confessor, but later was held by Alwold the Chamberlain. Under William the Conqueror it was again attached to the king's farm by

The modern Bere Court, seen here in front view, c. 1904

Froger the sheriff. The larger portion of Pangbourne also belonged to Edward the Confessor, his under-tenant being one Baldwin. Miles Crispin held it in 1086 and, like all his lands, it later formed part of the honour of Wallingford. There are no records of Pangbourne for nearly a century, but in 1166 the name of Richer of Pangbourne appears among the knights of the honour of Wallingford as one holding a knight's fee.

The earliest parish priest recorded is William, Chaplain of Pangbourne, mentioned in a charter of 1175 granting land at Streatley to Reading Abbey. This abbey was founded in 1121 by Henry I who had a great affection for it, richly endowing it with property which included the manor of Pangbourne.

In 1126 the manor and estate were given by Bingham, Bishop of Salisbury, to the Abbey of Reading and until the Reformation the estate was held by the mitred abbots of Reading as their country seat in the thirteenth and fourteenth centuries. A manor house at Bere Court exists today, about a mile and a half south-west of the village, its Georgian façade of red brick concealing parts of greater antiquity. In its early days Bere Court was undoubtedly of palatial proportions and appointment. The buildings associated with the manor have long since disappeared but a reminder of this period came to light hundreds of years later. A beautiful illuminated copy of the second edition of Wycliffe's Bible and a nun's Book of Hours were found in a prayer cell in the basement of the manor. Both were in perfect condition.

At the Dissolution of the Monasteries the estate and manor were given by Edward VI to John Dudley, Duke of Northumberland, who was beheaded in 1553. Tradition has it that the last Abbot of Reading, Hugh Cook Faringdon, was hiding there in a secret chamber when he was taken prisoner. He was a man of fine character but when he opposed Henry VIII's unscrupulous policies, trumped up evidence was brought against him and he was hanged, drawn and quartered outside the gates of his own Abbey in 1539. In 1563 Queen Elizabeth granted the manor of Pangbourne to Thomas Weldon, treasurer of the household, and his son Francis, subject to a lease of twenty-one years made by Queen Mary to Sir Francis Englefield.

In 1613 Francis Weldon sold the manor to Sir John Davis. John Davis had arrived at the Court of Queen Elizabeth in 1588 and became a follower of Robert Devereux, second Earl of Essex. In 1596 he took part in an expedition to Cadiz led by Essex and Admiral

A view of the rear of the modern Bere Court in 1920

Lord Howard to harass Spanish shipping preparing to attack England and for his part in this expedition he was knighted in the field by Essex himself. In 1600 Sir John was implicated in a plot led by Essex against Queen Elizabeth but the rebellion was discovered and Essex, together with four of his conspirators, was condemned to death. Two were beheaded, two hung, drawn and quartered but others, including Sir John, and for reasons not now known, obtained royal pardons and their lives were spared. Sir John bought Bere Court in 1613. He planned that the manor should become a hospital for wounded soldiers if his son died before him but as this did not happen his plan came to nothing. Sir John died at Bere Court in 1625 and there is a large monument to his memory in the parish church of St James the Less. After his death the Manor passed to his heir John II, who was himself later knighted. In 1671, a year after the house had been largely rebuilt, it was bought by John Breedon who became patron of the living.

The Breedon family, Lords of the Manor of Pangbourne for almost 200 years, owned the manor until the Breedon Estate was sold in 1894. John Breedon was a highly respected member of the Ironmongers' Company. In 1675 he became High Sheriff of Berkshire and on the 23 February of that year, the Court voted him, 'In remembrance of his many kindnesses, and willing to do him pleasure, a pipe of the best Canary that could be bought'. He was a Master of the Company for the year 1680 and although in ill-health was again elected in July 1685. A deputation went down to Bere Court to acquaint him of this but found him 'in great bodily weaknesse'. He was unable to attend at the Hall on Master's or Confirmation Day (the second Thursday in July) and at the next following Court (18 August) a letter from him was read declining office 'on account of his extreame weaknesse and bodily infirmitie'. The next line after the entry of this letter in the Court Book records 'Memo this day arrives the sorrowful newes of his decease'.

A cartouche on the south wall of the chancel in the parish church catalogues the virtues of this first John Breedon in the rather florid language of those days:

> Compassionate reader, beneath this monument lies ye body of JOHN BREEDON ESQRE, who (if thou hast any value for vertue) deserv's thy share of wonder and lamentation for the irreparable loss which the world sustains by ye death of soe great, soe good a man, whose exemplary piety, unshaken loyalty, profuse charity, and generous hospitality, will render his name precious to the

latest posterity. He was most just and righteous in all his dealings, curteous, affable and obliging in all his conversations, patient under his sufferings, and honourably esteem'd by all mankind, unblameable in his life, and full of glorious satisfaction in his last moment. He surrendered his pious soule August the 16th 1685 in the 64th yeare of his age.

In his will dated 24 March 1684, John Breedon devised 'a tenement with about half-an-acre of land enclosed with a flint wall to be a free school habitation for a schoolmaster' and gave as an endowment to the said school house:

> the yearly rent charge or sum of £40 per.an. to be raised free of all taxes out his estate in Pangbourne. In trust £25 per.an. thereof for the livelihood of the schoolmaster to be from time to time placed and put in by the Lord of the Manor, which schoolmaster is to teach without charge boys of the said parish 'especially the poorer sort of them', not exceeding twelve in number, in the Church Catechism now used as by law established, and also in other the true and orthodox principles of the Christian religion, which boys are to be chosen into the school by the Lord of the Manor. And £15 thereof to be employed towards placing to apprentice a boy in every two or three years.

What was this school building now houses Percy Stone's shop in Reading Road and the old entrance porch of the school is still to be seen. The endowment is still used for educational purposes.

As a family the Breedons were not blessed with many sons. John Breedon and his son, John I, were childless and nephews and distant relatives became their heirs. John IV had one son, also called John (V), but he, having no son of his own, named the son of his brother-in-law, Henry Symonds, as his heir. This next 'John' changed his name to John Symonds VI and was succeeded by his son, John VII. His heir, John VIII, died twenty-two days after his father in 1842 and was the last of the Breedon line.

They were a great influence in the village; four Breedons were Rectors of the parish church of St James the Less – Thomas Breedon 1705–17, John Symonds Breedon 1796–1817, Henry Breedon 1817–45 and Arthur William Breedon 1847–57. The sale of the Breedon estate in 1894 took place following the death in 1892 of Mrs Elizabeth Julia Breedon, widow of the Revd Henry Breedon.

It is recorded that the private chapel at the manor was demolished in 1802.

The Breedon family were Lords of the Manor of Bere Court from 1671 until 1894, when their freehold estate of 1848 acres was auctioned in the Small Town Hall in Reading on 17 July of that year. The income from the estate at this time was quoted as being £2,611. The new owner was Reginald de la Bere, who later sold it to Mr George Booth Tate of the Tate and Lyle sugar company in 1904. The manor has changed hands several times in this century and was bought by Mr Christopher Tucker in 1980. The modern Bere Court is privately owned and not open to the public.

— 2 —

The Parish Church of St James the Less

In the older part of the village, opposite a row of sixteenth-century cottages, stands the parish church of St James the Less. It is an elegant church with the battlements around its square tower dominating the sky line and the building itself serene among the gravestones as the traffic rumbles by.

Although it is not known exactly when the first church was built in Pangbourne it is certainly the second and, perhaps, the third church on this site. The parish registers date from 1556, the first entry being a marriage on 20 April of that year. Pangbourne is one of only twenty-six churches in the whole of England dedicated to St James the Less and most of the others have a joint dedication with St Philip. St James, often recognized as one of Jesus' brothers, is said to have met a martyr's death. From an early description he must have been a very strange character bearing no resemblance to the fine young man portrayed in the window on the north wall of the church. 'He never shaved, never cut his hair, never used any bath, he never wore sandals, never used any other clothes than one single linen garment. He prostrated so much in prayer that the skin of his knees and forehead was hardened like to camel's hoofs.'

The red brick tower was built in 1718 and there is a model of this early church in the vestry which shows a building of mixed provenance. Some of the windows are certainly not of medieval origin and may well be contemporaneous with the present pulpit which is Jacobean and came from an older church on the same site. By Victorian times the building, built of flint and clunch, a hard form of chalk which has a limited life when exposed to the weather, was in a parlous state.

Pangbourne parish church of St James the Less before the alterations and rebuilding of 1865/6

In 1865 the Rector, the Revd Robert Finch, had the church examined by Mr W.H. Woodman, an architect from Reading, who reported that 'the dilapidation of the building had very far advanced and that he had never examined a church that as a whole was in a worse condition for the performance of religious worship; there was a total absence of any features of historical or architectural interest in the church'. He recommended that the nave of the church, which was supposed to be about 200 years old, should be rebuilt and the work began in March of that year.

In taking down the old church it was surprising that no traces of great antiquity could be discovered. One or two broken pieces of stone which might have been portions of Early English windows, a few George III coins and some of a later date were all that was found. The only things that could be preserved were the oak pulpit and all that remained of the chalk monument to Sir John Davis. The new church was built of knapped flint with Bath stone dressings and moulding of the Decorated period and a chancel that extended further east over the existing graveyard. This extension was not well supported since in this decade a considerable sum has had to be raised to meet the cost of underpinning. The interior of the church was designed to convey the impression of a building constructed over a period of time like most medieval churches. The nave arcade is Transitional whilst the chancel with its naturalistic carving of the capitals and around the chancel arch is Decorated, a period approximately 100 years later. The roofs are supported on cusped scissor trusses and that of the chancel on arch braced trusses, the arrises decorated with beautiful carvings of riverside flowers and plants. The chancel arcade, enclosing the organ, is supported on carved corbels and a capital which is itself supported on a polished granite pillar, presented to the rebuilt church by the architect, Mr W.H. Woodman. The Revd Robert Finch who had initiated the rebuilding described the new church as 'at once a credit to the architect and the diocese, as well as a great boon to the parishioners.'

On 22 June 1866, only fifteen months after work had commenced, the Bishop of Oxford officiated at the reopening of the church and consecrated a piece of ground measuring 847 square yards which was added to the churchyard. The total cost of rebuilding was £3,202 2s. 4d.

The red brick tower has been mellowed by sun, wind and rain for over 270 years and forms a striking contrast to the flint and stone dressings of the rest of the church. The walls of the tower are 3 ft

The parish church, c. 1884

thick and of clunch with a facing of 9 in brickwork and the battle-
mented parapet is faced with stone dressings. There are a number of
inscribed bricks and stones set into the fabric of the west face of the
tower. The west window, below the stones, is a rather poor, plain,
square opening with unmoulded mullions and transoms of wood. On
the south face just above the doorway some of the bricks are
inscribed – I.B.1718: H.B.1718: Thomas Buckeridge 1718. The
Buckeridge family was widely spread in Berkshire and Oxfordshire in
the seventeenth and eighteenth centuries.

The tower contains a peal of six bells cast in 1720 by Abraham
Rudhall of Gloucester bearing the following inscriptions:

1st	When we ring I sweetly sing. A.R.1720
2nd	God preserve the Church. Amen. A.R.1720
3rd	Peace and good neighbourhood. A.R.1720
4th	Abr. Rudhall of Gloucester, bell founder 1720
5th	Prosperity to all our benefactors. A.R.1720
6th	The Revnd Ben Loveling, Rectr. Wm Loader and Richd Wilder, Churchwardens, 1720

The tenor bell, the note of which is A flat, is said to weigh nine and a half hundredweight. An unusual feature of the bells is that they are hung on the diagonal from corner to corner of the tower. They were put into repair in 1876 at a cost of £68.

A new organ having 12 stops and 498 pipes built by H Wedlake of Regent's Park, London, was installed in 1882 at a cost, allowing for re-use of pipes from the previous organ, of £3,185 14s.10d. Its successor, the present organ, was built by George Sixsmith of Mossley, Lancashire in 1983 at a cost of £26,600. The pipes of the Wedlake organ were revoiced with additional pipework to provide more adequate manual choruses. The swell box of the old organ was improved to give better projection of sound.

The church clock was the gift of Antrum Woolford in 1789 whose name with that date appears on the dial on the east face of the tower but not on the more easily seen south facing one. The east facing dial is higher, perched a little uneasily at the top of the belfry louvre. It had to be moved to this position during rebuilding because the roof of the new nave came a lot higher than the old. The clock was repaired in 1880 at a cost of £40 13s. 6d. and again in 1990 at a cost of £700. Behind the organ is the large seventeenth-century monument to Sir John Davis made of chalk from local Shooters Hill. He lies clad in armour with his two wives beside him dressed 'in their usuall habbitts' and his dog at his feet. Under the tomb are statuettes of his son and daughter and on top sits a model of a skull, quite a common feature in those days, to remind people of their mortality.

The seventeenth-century monument to Sir John Davis

Unfortunately, after more than 350 years the chalk has crumbled and the little dog and the heads of Sir John's son and daughter are missing.

A large floor tablet outside the vestry is in memory of Jane Robinson wife of Thos Robinson 'Chiefe Prothonotary of HM

Court of Common Pleas' who died at Bere Court:

> in ye 49 yeare of her age by a cancer in her breast which she suf-
> fered with an invincible patience to be cut of, and survived onely
> 6 months after, dyed on ye 22 November 1665 and was here
> interred December ye 8th to whose deare memorie her most
> indulgent husband hath erected this adjoiyning monument.

One of the seven hatchments to the Breedon family at the rear of the parish church

Perhaps this is the first record-ed evidence of a mastectomy. There is another monument in Latin to this brave woman on the north wall of the church by the well known sculptor Thos Stanton of Holborn.

The seven hatchments at the back of the church are those of the Breedon family, lords of the manor of Pangbourne from 1671 until the nineteenth century. A hatchment is a lozenge shaped piece of wood painted with the arms of local gentry made at the time of their death. Initially they were placed on the front of the house as a sign of mourning and then, after a suitable period, removed to the parish church where they remained. These hatchments are particularly interesting as few churches have so many relating to one family. There are also eight memorial tablets to the Breedon family on the walls of the chancel and outside the vestry.

Near the window on the north wall is a plaque to Arthur Sackville Trevor Griffith-Boscawen, Privy Councillor, soldier and sometime Cabinet Minister. He was also a County Councillor in Pangbourne and died here in 1946.

In the south-west corner of the church near the door to the tower are three plaques. One commemorates Dr Kidgell, a much loved surgeon in this village. Another is to a member of the family made famous by Sir Edwin Lutyens, the architect who among other things designed the Cenotaph. Next to these is a plaque to the memory of Sir Benjamin Baker, who lived in Pangbourne and designed the

The old forge opposite the church, c. 1919

famous Forth Bridge, a span of which is represented. He was also one of the principal engineers of much of the London Underground system.

The beautiful east window by Karl Parsons is one of the best examples of his work. It was given by Sir George and Lady Armstrong in memory of their son, George Carlyon Armstrong, their nephew, Philip Armstrong and all men of the parish who gave their lives for their country in the Great War of 1914–18.

The window on the south wall is in memory of Emilie Helena (Willoughby) wife of Major General Thomas Waddington of the East India Company and the window on the north wall in memory of the Hillcoat family.

Opposite the church is the old forge which was owned by the Cox family for generations. At one time Mr Cox held the keys of the church so he could take care of the church clock and the dip in the roof of the forge enabled him to keep an eye on the clock while he was at work.

— 3 —

The Rector and the Miller

In the latter part of the nineteenth century two men were prominent in the life of the village of Pangbourne. One was the Revd Robert Finch and the other was Robert Stone, miller of Pangbourne. They were strong characters who left their mark on the village and whose paths crossed many times, often with fiery results. A short description of the lives and times of these two men gives an interesting insight into the life of the village at that time.

Sheep in the square, probably in the 1870s

The Revd Finch was responsible for instigating the rebuilding of the church in 1866, and it was his initiative and energy that ensured there would continue to be a parish church at Pangbourne for generations to come. But his incumbency was far from harmonious. He was a dominant character with a 'Lord of the Manor' air about him which often brought him at loggerheads with his churchwardens and parishioners. His vestry meetings were reported in the local press with headlines such as, 'Stormy Vestry Meeting', 'Another Remarkable Meeting' and 'Another Excited Vestry Meeting – an enquiry to be asked for'. This last headline refers to an enquiry into the endowments, objects and circumstances of the parish charities which was held in December 1890 with the inspector under the Charities Commission, Whitehall, in attendance. The Breedon School charity was the first under discussion. 'Why', the inspector asked, 'were only six free boys now attending the school when John Breedon's will of 1684 stated that free places should be allocated to twelve?' A great argument followed over the delicacy of the school-master's conscience that would not allow him to teach boys who had not been baptised and the Rector's apparent unwillingness to let the vacancies be more widely known to those eligible. The Revd Finch said that applications were to be reviewed the following January and the rest of the evening was spent in discussing finances. The meeting, reported in detail in the *Reading Observer*, had lasted seven hours.

A booklet entitled *A Short Account of the Parish of Pangbourne* written by the Revd Finch in 1890, gives a valuable glimpse into the life of the parish at that time. There is a plaque to the memory of him and his wife above the pulpit in the church he rebuilt with such pride. His tomb is in the churchyard beside the lamp-post behind the tower and beside him is the grave of Elizabeth Charles, 'faithful and valued servant in the family of Mr Finch of Pangbourne Rectory for 66 years, who died in 1870 aged 80 years'.

Robert Stone, parish councillor and churchwarden was born at High Wycombe in 1852. He was in

Robert Stone the miller as a young man

many ways an example of a Victorian ideal; a successful man whose life and success was based on high ethics, hard work and a certain benevolence to his fellow men. He came to Pangbourne in 1871 to become miller at Pangbourne Mill which stood just past the Cross Keys, opposite the cottages at the foot of Pangbourne Hill. As he was only a young man of nineteen, his father Alfred Stone was tenant. But not for long. Robert, a slight man, only 5 ft 2 in in height and weighing under 10 stone, made up for his lack of stature with abundant energy and an untiring capacity for hard work. In his diaries, written between 1869 and 1882, there are numerous entries like: 'Work from 8.30 to 8.15', 'Worked the mill till 10.30', 'Up at six, busy at the mill all day', 'returned to work the water down at night until 2.30 am'.

He describes riding to Bradfield to buy hens and a cockerel for 26*s*. and making a sty of bricks for his six little pigs. Almost daily he sent letters by the penny post to his sweetheart Rachel Cooper at High Wycombe. With her black hair and gentle blue eyes Rachel was quite a beauty and it was said that Robert had first been attracted to her by the fresh white stockings she wore to church each Sunday. On 11 February 1873 he 'bought Rachel an engagement ring with pearls

Children in the village square, c. 1919

and turquoises to give her on the occasion of my 21st birthday'. They were married at High Wycombe on 15 October of that year, when the bride wore a lavender silk dress with shawl bonnet and gold drop earrings. Robert's rather serious account of the day in his diary ends with: 'Rachel packed her remaining clothes and wedding presents which are very numerous and we left together by last train reaching Pangbourne safely at 9.15. Went to bed at 11.30.' The following day, 'Rose at 7, Rachel busy clearing up the house all day.' They lived at the Mill House, still there today with the mill stream running through the garden.

Rachel bore Robert eleven children, the family prospered and in 1888 Tidmarsh Mill was added to his business. In 1894 Robert achieved his ambition when, at the sale of the Bere Court estate, he bought and became owner of Pangbourne Mill with residence, meadow and fishery.

At that time there were six working mills on the River Pang: Pangbourne, Tidmarsh, Maidenhatch, Bradfield, Stanford Dingley and Frilsham. It was not until 1929, eleven years after his death, that Pangbourne Mill was closed and converted to the present water pumping station.

In April 1890 Robert Stone was elected churchwarden. On voting day the village was placarded with large posters inviting people to 'Vote for Stone and for the poor people to have coals', while men paraded the street carrying boards bearing the same message. According to the *Reading Observer* 'the election was carried on without the slightest approach to ill-feeling but it was evident on all hands that it was not a fight between Mr Stone and Mr Mortimore [his opponent] but, to quote a leading inhabitant "A fight of the people against the parson." The poll closed at 2 o'clock and the result: Stone 82: Mortimore 49: was hailed with great cheering and Mr Stone was hoisted in the arms of several of his supporters and carried triumphantly through the village'. At a victory dinner at The Elephant, Robert Stone proposed a toast to 'The Workers' to which Mr Cox replied with a toast to 'The Overseers'.

Robert and the Rector were continually at loggerheads and at one point their exchanges became so violent that Robert marched his entire family out of church and into chapel. On their arrival at chapel the pew was so crammed that two of the boys were sent up into the balcony where they amused themselves by dropping pellets of paper on to the heads of the people below.

Robert's involvement with the community brought plenty of

Robert and Rachel Stone with their ten children, c. 1900

frustrations – like the problem with the locked gates. In a letter to the editor of *The Reading Observer* in 1890 Robert complains that the parish clerk not only locked the churchyard gates after services but took the key home with him to the other end of the village. Consequently people visiting the graves of their relatives after church were locked in and unable to get out of the churchyard. One Sunday a group of ladies and children who had been loitering in the churchyard could only leave by climbing over the wall. Owing to the kindness of a neighbour, who brought a chair, the children were able to get away but the ladies stayed in the churchyard until, 'after an exercise of patience, the parish clerk made his appearance, keys in hand, and put an end to the dilemma'. 'I ask, Sir,' Robert continues, 'is it right that we who have our relatives buried in God's acre should not have free access to it at all reasonable times! My growing daughters are often obliged to climb the wall to put wreaths on our grave . . . but I shall not allow this much longer before I take strong measures to remove the difficulty and prove my right. The sheep are, I am glad to say, temporarily, I trust permanently, removed from the churchyard.' Robert duly proved his rights by removing the lock on the gates so that parishioners should have free access to the churchyard at all times.

Strong measures were again needed in 1896. Under the heading 'Exciting Scene at Pangbourne' *The Reading Observer* reports:

Village children, c. 1900

There was great excitement in Pangbourne yesterday evening week, when, in the presence of a large number of villagers an obstruction to an alleged right of way was removed. Visitors to Pangbourne are familiar with the Green Lane which from time immemorial has been a public thoroughfare and was, indeed, the old turnpike road to Bradfield. It is also the road which centuries ago was used by the monks of Reading Abbey on their way to their retreat at Bere Court. At the sale of the Breedon estate a Mr Coulter bought 'Courtlands' which is bounded on one side by the Green Lane. Yesterday week it was discovered that the gate had been fastened with a padlock and 'decorated' with barbed wire. This was naturally held by the inhabitants to be an infringement of public rights. Accordingly at the quarterly meeting of the Parish Council, yesterday week, Mr Cox brought forward the question as a matter of urgency, and it was decided to ask Mr Stone to remove the obstruction, a task which that gentleman readily undertook. The Council meeting was adjourned, and the members went to see their orders carried out, being accompanied by a large number of villagers. Mr Stone had

Whitchurch Road showing the premises of the Tidbury brothers who recorded late Victorian Pangbourne in picture postcards

meanwhile armed himself with a formidable crowbar, a hammer and a chisel. Arrived at the spot Mr Stone and his many willing helpers proceeded to forcibly remove the padlock and the barbed wire. Amid cheers and the encouraging shouts of the onlookers the work proceeded, and in a few minutes the gate swung back to the accompaniment of more cheers. The gate has not since been locked.

Robert Stone died in 1918, aged sixty-six, and his wife, Rachel, eleven years later. They are buried in a corner of the churchyard beside the wall of the old Elephant Hotel and beside them lie two of their daughters. The Stone family business continues today as Percy Stone Ltd in the High Street.

— 4 —

The Growth of the Village

In 1801 the population of Pangbourne was 593 with 131 families. The census return for that year makes interesting reading.

   Gentry: 15 male, 20 female, 35 in 5 homes
   Trade: 161 male, 154 female, 315 in 48 homes
   Husbandry: 120 male, 123 female, 243 in 25 homes

In 1851 the population had risen to 800 but only 219 were entirely dependent on agriculture. The rest of the workers included crafts-men, the miller and his men, professionals, sawyers and woodmen, railwaymen and boatbuilders. There were 58 servants including 3 ostlers.

The arrival of Isambard Kingdom Brunel's Great Western Railway in 1840 changed the face of the quiet village of Pangbourne. During the great excavations, for which Irish labourers were employed, traces of a bygone age were unearthed. In the deep cutting through Shooters Hill, among the relics found were an iron spear-head 23 in in length, a Roman coin of Constantine, urns, more coins, and spear-heads and nearly a hundred skeletons, lying in rows, probably the site of a Roman burial ground. There was also a structure resembling the foundations of a lime kiln containing a large quantity of charcoal and burnt human bones.

When at last the railway was completed, a new prosperity began. The beautiful stretches of the River Thames, now only a short jour-ney from London, became increasingly popular as a place where people who worked in the city could spend a peaceful weekend. Artists, writers and anglers descended on the village alighting at the

Workmen repairing a hole in the Reading Road near the junction with Horseshoe Road, c. 1900

Pangbourne station, c. 1864

Pangbourne Station around 1900 after the addition of the footbridge

Queuing for bread at the bakers during the First World War

Pangbourne Post Office and all the staff posing in about 1900

new station described as 'a neat and commodious structure, some-what in the style of a Swiss cottage, with Elizabethan windows. The projecting shed, while it imparts additional importance to the build-ing, affords increased accommodation to the public who, indeed, have no reason to complain of inattention to their comforts on this railway . . .' But comfort was hardly experienced by the second class passengers who travelled in carriages resembling the inside of a stage coach with plain wooden seats and although there was a roof over-head, there was no glass in the windows so that passengers sitting near the sides were uncomfortably exposed to the wind and the rain. Still the people came. As Pangbourne increased in popularity, shops, banks and service industries started to appear and in 1862 a gas works was built beside the railway bridge over Station Road on the site now occupied by Sycamore Court. The river became an angling centre, attracting fishermen from far and wide to the quiet of the river bank.

After the sale of the Breedon estate in 1894 development of the 1,848 acres changed the face of Pangbourne even more. Shooters Hill, an elevation overlooking the river at Pangbourne Reach, said to have got its name through having been an archery practice ground,

The Boat House, Pangbourne   Photo by Tidbury

The boat houses outside the Swan Hotel. Boats like the one in the foreground were popular for holiday hire and with the tarpaulin folded down could be slept in

Shooters Hill and the 'Seven Deadly Sins'

was a prime site for development. Set back from the road with the railway embankment behind it and river frontage before, are seven elegant houses built in 1896 and known locally as the 'Seven Deadly Sins'. The large building on the corner of what is now Hartslock Court was originally Shooters Hill House, built in 1898 and designed by the architect Leonard Stokes for D.H. Evans, founder of the well-known London store. Mr Evans lived there for many years and although he took an active part in the community some people never forgave him for 'scooping out seven holes in the side of Shooters Hill and stuffing them with the "Deadly Sins"'. Shooters Hill House is now divided into three, a part of which contains the Masonic Hall. The little thatched Shooters Hill Cottage was once an ale house called 'The Hole in the Wall'.

In the late 1890s a manual fire engine was bought for the village at a cost of £130, including uniforms and equipment. The engine was kept at what is now the entrance to the car park of Percy Stone's shop in the High Street. When a fire started, a maroon was exploded which brought the volunteer firemen running from all parts of the village. The fire station was later moved further down the Reading Road to the site which is now the Library and later still to its present site in Horseshoe Road.

By the turn of the century grand houses for the wealthy and more modest ones for the workers were springing up everywhere and by 1901 the population had risen to 1,235. While some welcomed this new prosperity others were loud in their disapproval. In 1899 two anonymous 'Visitors' wrote bitterly to *The South Bucks Free Press*:

What a remarkable change has been wrought at Pangbourne in the last few years! Shooters Hill is lost to the public, villas or bungalows have been erected at the foot of the famous hill, and in the village large and handsome shops, some worthy of a town, have been erected while the Old Elephant Hotel has given place to a large and commodious structure. Hitherto it has been the custom of the road authorities after wet weather to scrape the mud off the village streets on Saturdays and leave the mud on the sides of the roads until the following week. In the darkness of the village no one can see where these heaps of mud are. Would it not be better for the Surveyor only to have scraped up what mud he could cart away on the same day, and also employ a boy every Saturday to pick up the odd pieces of paper that are left to blow about the village streets all day on Sundays?

Paddling in the Pang at Pangbourne.

The River Pang was a popular paddling place for village children. It rarely contains as much water as this today

On enquiring into why the village was so dark at night I was informed that the local Gas Company asked the Parish Council the enormous sum of £3 each for 20 lamps per annum for public lighting. This 'libel' offer was, of course, not accepted. The church clock (the only public clock in the parish) has recently been from five to ten minutes behind the railway time which has often caused much inconvenience to intending railway travellers.

It was with regret that I heard of one retrograde movement. The village boys have for very many years bathed in the Thames

Pangbourne Reach, c. 1887, seen from Shooters Hill. The house in the foreground was the Hole in the Wall Inn. Notice the gipsy caravans drawn up along the Streatley road

The bathing pool and changing hut

in the Lock pool and used to dress on an island in the centre of the pool screened by the natural sedge and trees. Many a Pangbourne lad has learned the art of swimming at this beautiful spot. But a London gentleman came down, bought the land on the opposite bank, and turned the poor little boys off the island. Is it too much to ask that the island be restored to the boys for bathing purposes?

A week later the second 'Visitor' wrote:

'Old Pangbourne' I will call it – was a choice chronicle of an age which knew not the tactics to which we descend today in our attempt to ease the burdens of life. The habits, occupation and home of the villager were ancient to a nicety; there could be found here, on the banks of the river, every rural complement which weary minds seek – the peacefulness which modern improvements fail to give. Pangbourne remained and nature was practically undisturbed. Then came the rush of speculators and builders. Pangbourne came under the muck rake. For the sake of gold the highest recommendations of Pangbourne were desecrated under what we call 'commercial enterprises'. Jerry builders and local parasites, fresh faces, and the newest of London

Two views of the Square and High Street in the early years of the century

Swimmers diving from Whitchurch Bridge into the Thames. There are still people living in Pangbourne today who can remember doing this

'fishermen' have given us a taste of modernising. The thatched cottage is doomed or patched and the meadows are sacrificed to hold red bricks, bad mortar, and worse drainage. The new villas at the foot of Shooter's Hill are undoubtedly smart and up-to-date, but what a sad apology for the Shooter's Hill we formerly knew!

The greed for gold will stop at nothing – men in their eagerness violate nature's best work and when they leave it no amount of 'moderning' can equal the original masterpiece. And so with old Pangbourne. There is a Pangbourne of today and another which lives in the memory.

— 5 —

Pangbourne Schools

One of the grand houses built at the end of the nineteenth century was Clayesmore, the mansion that is now Pangbourne College. Standing a mile south of the village off Bere Court Road, this elegant building of red brick with a massive stone porch tower was built and designed in a William and Mary style by Sir John Belcher in 1897–8. In 1917 the mansion became the Nautical College, an establishment founded by Sir Thomas Lane Devitt and his son Sir Philip Devitt with the approval of the Admiralty to educate and train boys for both the

Clayesmore, the mansion that became the Nautical College

A modern print of Pangbourne College by Mick Ewins

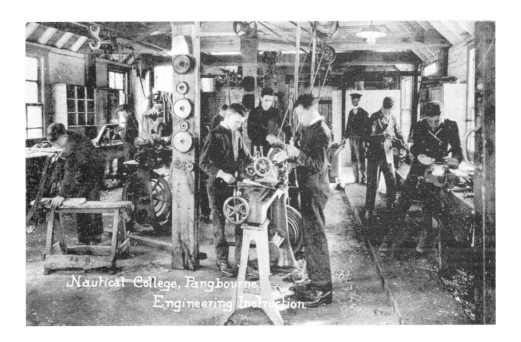

Pupils at the Nautical College in about 1920

Royal and Merchant Navies. The founders, however, intended that the education provided was to be suitable also for any boy who subsequently decided not to go to sea. Thus, through the years many pupils become officers not only in the Royal and Merchant Navies but also in the Army and Royal Air Force. In 1968 Pangbourne College ceased to be a nautical college and is now a public school for boys. The school stands in grounds of 250 acres and retains a river frontage on the Thames of over 100 yards, with a large house, boat-house and craft of all sizes, from large motor-boats to sailing dinghies. Its history as a nautical college means that rowing and sailing are major sports at the school, and in 1971 the college First Eight won the Princess Elizabeth Cup at Henley Royal Regatta and in 1990 the college First Six became the National Sailing Champions.

The old parish school, known as the Breedon School, was, by 1863, deemed to be very ill-adapted to the needs of the parish and steps were taken to improve the building which seems originally to have been a row of four cottages. The old school room, barely 7 ft high, was taken down and replaced with a large new room and the master's house was also made fit for habitation. Further additions for infants were added between 1873–5 and further improvements were made in 1883. In 1900, its successor, the Council School, where

The Oram's greengrocers shop about 1915, now NatWest Bank

pupils paid 4*d.* a week for their tuition, was built on Pangbourne Hill and was attended by the local children until the present Pangbourne Junior School was built at the far end of the village in the late 1970s.

The old school lay on the line of a proposed bypass and when the plan was formally dropped in the 1980s the site was redeveloped for housing as Stokes View.

Beryl Cox, a former pupil of the school recalls:

It was not a hazardous journey walking to school in the late 1920s and early 1930s. There was little traffic and still quite a few horses and carts. The village school was then situated on Pangbourne Hill. It had a loud bell which rang in the mornings and again at lunchtime (I think it was really to hurry the children along). On our way to school we would stop a few minutes at Cox's blacksmiths and watch a horse being shod. When Mr Cox put the new red-hot shoe on the horse's hoof, there was a puff of blue smoke, a sizzling noise and a not very nice smell. The memory is still very vivid. It always amazed me that the horse never seemed to mind the operation. Occasionally, we would catch a glimpse of Kenneth Grahame, coming out of his gate at Church Cottage. He was a distinguished looking gentleman. Major Harbor, the Headmaster at that time was a very nice, family man (but a disciplinarian) and a Christian. The

The Square in about 1950

teaching staff were all very nice, caring people who had the children's welfare at heart. Reading, writing and arithmetic (as it was then) were important, likewise, English, spelling and memory training. The school had a boys' football team and a girls' netball team. Bullying seemed to be unheard of in those days. Some children were able to sit for a scholarship to a Grammar or Secondary School. Children who did not have this opportunity left school at fourteen but were able to read, write, spell and add up. That was a lot to be thankful for. What bliss schooldays were!

In the 1930s and 1940s small traders flourished in Pangbourne. There were several of each type of shop to choose from, including three butchers, three bakeries and two dairies. The Home Farm Dairy in the High Street and Mr Harper's dairy at the far end of the village vied with each other for custom and it was a common sight to see two of Mr Harper's daughters trundling a milk churn on a trolley up the village street morning and afternoon. In the 1920s milk was

Fisherman's Cottage, c. 1887

Harper's Dairy delivery cart

10*d*. a quart. The sign of a spinning wheel on the wall over a shop near the Post Office is a reminder of the days when a group of Pangbourne ladies ran the Spinning Wheel Tea Shop, where afternoon teas were served at the price of 2*s*. The Constitution Club above the row of shops in Whitchurch Road was a centre of social activities with dances, parties, meetings and a place to gather after the pubs were closed.

— 6 —

Notable Village Residents

Throughout the years a number of notable people have either lived or stayed at Pangbourne.

During the eighteenth century the dramatist Thomas Morton, who lived in Pangbourne for thirty-five years, produced the play *Speed the Plough* in which the formidable Mrs Grundy is never seen but her opinions on decorum are fearfully anticipated. His son, John Morton was born here in 1811 and produced nearly a hundred farces of which *Box and Cox* is best remembered because it became a milestone to success for Sir Arthur Sullivan, who set it to music.

William Tufnell LeQuex, popular writer of sensational stories of crime and espionage, lived at the house in Reading Road which became the Spinning Wheel. He died in October 1927.

Arthur Sackville Trevor Griffith-Boscawen, Privy Councillor and sometime Cabinet Minister, was also a county councillor in Pangbourne and died here in 1946.

The actor George Arliss lived at a house in Reading Road called 'The Myrtles'.

D.H. Lawrence and his wife also stayed at 'The Myrtles' in 1919 when the owner of a cottage at Hermitage, where they had been staying, 'turned them out' as Lawrence put it, and they were desperate for somewhere to live. In July of that year he wrote to a friend, 'pleasant house – hate Pangbourne itself – nothing happens'. At the end of August they were back at Hermitage.

Sir Benjamin Baker, who designed the famous Forth Bridge and also Mortimer Menpes, Anglo-Australian painter and etcher, both lived in the village in the late nineteenth century.

Perhaps the best known name to be associated with Pangbourne

Kenneth Grahame (1912), from the drawing by John S. Sargent

was Kenneth Grahame, author of the children's classic, *Wind in the Willows*. Kenneth Grahame was born in Edinburgh in 1859. His mother died when he was a child and, together with his brothers and sister, he went to live with his grandmother at the Thames-side village of Cookham Dean. He was later to become Secretary of the Bank of England and write several books for children as well as the one for which he is famous. In 1899 he married Elspeth Thomson when they were both forty. Elspeth, who was something of an eccentric, chose to be married in an old muslin dress with a daisy chain round her neck rather than wear her expensive wedding gown. Their marriage was not an easy one, Elspeth enjoying an active social life with the literary figures of the day and Kenneth preferring a quieter life and time with

Church Cottage where the Grahames lived. The conical-roofed building was an old village lock-up, used as a toolshed by Kenneth Grahame

his small circle of friends. Their son, Alistair (nicknamed 'Mouse') was born in 1900. Blind in one eye and not overbright, he was unhappy at his public school and at Oxford, unable to live up to his mother's inflated image of him as a brilliant and socially acceptable scholar. His father made his son into a sort of dream child and it was for him that Kenneth wrote *The Wind in the Willows,* starting it as a bedtime story and carrying it on in serial letters. If the governess had not kept the letters the book might never have been published. While a student at Oxford disaster struck. The unhappy Alistair, aged twenty-one, was found dead on a railway line and at the inquest a verdict of accidental death was recorded. It was after this tragedy that the Grahames came to live at Pangbourne in 1924. Church Cottage adjoining the church looks much as it did when they lived there, including the old village lock-up with grille window and tapering circular roof still in the garden in which it was enclosed when Riverview Road was developed in the late 1890s. An account of 1523 describes a village lock-up as being for the temporary custody of such as were 'caught in the act, or suspects, or drunks and rowdies'. Known as a lock-up, blind house, cage or clink it was not a gaol, the distinction being that the occupant was still to be brought to trial. In the Grahames' time it was used as a toolshed.

Pangbourne Reach, c. 1887

The river at Pangbourne is very similar to the stretch below Cookham Dean, the inspiration for his stories of the riverside creatures, and not, as is sometimes assumed locally, Pangbourne.

The Grahames were as eccentric as ever and could often be seen eating their lunch out of a paper bag on the porch of Church Cottage. Elspeth was by now a pale ghostly figure with fuzzy grey hair and disreputable clothes. She could be very charming and was extremely fond of children. Every Christmas she would give the schoolchildren a little present taking their names from the school register to make sure no one was missed out and making them line up at Church Cottage to receive their gift. Kenneth was a withdrawn but amiable old gentleman and can still be remembered striding through the village in his cloak, trilby hat and black and white check scarf with white hair flowing. He took long riverside walks or sat

Horse-drawn barges on the Thames below Shooters Hill in 1900

alone in his garden for hours on end and refused to have either a permanent servant or a telephone installed in the house. He was well known as an author of books and plays for both adults and children. These included *Pagan Papers* (1893), *Golden Age* (1895) and *Dream Days* (1898). His extremely successful *Wind in the Willows* (1908) was later also successful as the Christmas play, dramatized as T*oad of Toad Hall*, by A.A. Milne.

He died in 1932 from a cerebral haemorrhage. His funeral at St James the Less was described in *The Times* of 11 July of that year. 'The church was a marvellous sight – a blaze of glorious colour and sunshine – with masses of flowers, delphiniums and roses and willows gathered from the river that morning ... and perhaps the most touching thing of all were the flowers sent by children from all over the country with cards attached in a childish scrawl saying how much they loved him. The grave was lined with thousands of sweet peas and the scent was unforgettable.'

His body was later removed to Holywell Cemetery, Oxford where he now lies beside his son. The inscription on his stone reads, 'To the beautiful memory of Kenneth Grahame who passed the river on 6 July 1932 leaving childhood and literature the more blessed because of him'.

— 7 —

The River

The stretch of river at Pangbourne is one of the loveliest on the Thames and has always played an important part in the life of the village as a means of transport and a place of recreation. Pangbourne Reach where today the Pangbourne College boys can be seen practising their rowing skills was once the end of the journey for barges

Royal Engineers complete a pontoon bridge across the Thames during training in the First World War

The weir pool from Whitchurch Bridge. The Swan Inn is in the background and a landing-stage for the George Hotel is on the left

Troops train in bridge building in 1939

The final Bailey bridge built in May 1946 by 10 Training Battalion, Royal Engineers. This was the only time that the public were allowed to cross the river on one of these bridges

The weir and Swan Inn, c. 1887

preparing to unload their cargo at the wharf beside the Swan Hotel. This wharf and another wharf and boatyard just upstream from Whitchurch Bridge, have disappeared over recent years and the river traffic now consists of pleasure boats on cruises along the Thames.

In 1899 the bridge in the High Street over the river Pang adjoined a ford. The bridge was narrower than it is today but you can still see where horses and carts went into the water to swell the wood of the cartwheels and keep the rims tight.

During the First and Second World Wars the river at Pangbourne was used for army training purposes. American, Canadian, Australian and Royal Engineers, gained experience in building bailey and pontoon bridges. In the preparations for D-Day many bridges were built and dismantled again between Pangbourne Meadow and Thames Bank opposite. The troops under training were accommodated in Nissen huts in Coombe Park.

Pangbourne Meadow, now owned by the Parish Council, and the six acres of National Trust land beyond are for the public's enjoyment whether they are fishing, swimming, boating or walking along the towpath on the river bank.

The River Pang flowing through the water meadows that stretch from beyond the end of the Moors was higher than it is today and

The great flood of 1896

Construction of the iron bridge to Whitchurch in 1901

was a favourite bathing place for children who would picnic on its banks. The meadows are still enjoyed today by those who walk there and gather wild flowers by the way.

In years gone by the Thames Valley was often afflicted by winter floods, and Pangbourne village was no exception. The Great Flood in November 1894 was one of the highest that had been known for many years, probably since 1821. The river began to rise rapidly on Wednesday, 14 November and attained the highest point on Friday the 16th. The water reached half way across the road by the Elephant Hotel (now the Copper Inn) and extended to the Cross Keys Inn and the baker's shop opposite, where the water was 6–8 in deep in the sitting-room. At the Swan Hotel the water was 28 in deep in the bar and 25 in in the parlour where it poured out of the windows in a strong stream. Boats floated along the village street and at the boat house of E.J. Ashley the water mark registered 6 ft higher than the ordinary summer level. The river flooded again in 1947 and also in 1951, when it filled the cellars of the Swan and spoiled the beer.

In 1963 the river was frozen for miles around the village. Nowadays modern technology enables the river authority to exercise much better control of water and the risk of flooding in this part of the Thames Valley is very much reduced.

Whitchurch toll-gate

The Cross Keys Inn around 1900

Whitchurch Bridge

The south branch of that ancient road, the Ridgeway, dropped down to the Thames at Pangbourne and was one of the earliest crossing places into Oxfordshire, first by a ferry and later by the first of two wooden bridges. The Whitchurch Bridge Act of 1792 gave permission for the building of a bridge over the Thames from near the ferry in Pangbourne to Whitchurch in the county of Oxfordshire and required it to be a good substantial wooden bridge with abutments made of stone, brick or other material. A tollhouse or houses were to be constructed near the bridge. On its completion £350 was to be paid as compensation to the owners of the ferry and no one was allowed, under penalty of a fine, to ferry passengers across for hire or to cross the river by the weir. The profits taken were from the tolls which were originally:

For every person on foot	¹/₂d
For every horse, mare, gelding, or mule, laden or unladen, and not drawing	2d
For every ass, laden, drawing or not drawing	1¹/₂d
For every bull, ox, cow, steer, heifer or calf	2d
For every sheep or lamb	¹/₂d
For every boar, sow, or pig	¹/₂d
For every horse, mare, gelding, mule, or other beast, except asses, drawing any carriage	2d
For every carriage with two or more wheels 2d for each and every wheel	

No toll was to be charged for men or horses drawing vessels to Whitchurch Lock, or returning from drawing.

This bridge was replaced by a second wooden one in 1840. When this bridge in its turn showed signs of deterioration the present iron bridge was built in 1901.

Crossing the bridge is still subject to a toll. At the time of writing it is 6p for a car capable of carrying not more than eight passengers and light vehicles of less than 1.525 tonnes unladen weight. Larger vehicles pay 5p plus 5p per tonne or part of a tonne over 1 tonne unladen weight. A proposal for an increase in these charges is presently under consideration by the Department of Transport.

— 8 —

Hotels and Inns

The Copper Inn at the junction of the High Street and Station Road was formerly the Elephant and Castle and later just the Elephant (known locally as the Jumbo). Its name was changed to the Copper Inn in the mid-1960s. In the eighteenth century it was a coaching house where traders travelling along the old Roman road from Dorchester to Silchester stopped to change their horses.

The Elephant Hotel in 1887. Formerly the Elephant and Castle, it is now the Copper Inn

The railway arches in about 1884. It would not be safe to stand in the roadway like this today

When the crew of Admiral Nelson's ship *Victory* were paid off in 1815, his favourite coxswain, Thomas Carter, stayed at the Elephant and frittered away his prize money by lavishly entertaining his friends. The old man settled down at Pangbourne and when he died the landlord of the Elephant flew the Union Jack at half mast as a sign of mourning. The story goes that local people, usually associating flags with festivities, imagined the landlord was rejoicing at Carter's death and broke every window in the place! Thomas Carter was buried in Pangbourne churchyard with the Union Jack as a shroud but, sadly, there is no sign of his grave today. During alterations to the inn many old beams were exposed and it was clear that, as was common in those days, much of the wood was secondhand, possibly ship's timber. As Nelson's flagship at the battle of Copenhagen was *The Elephant* there has been speculation that both the original name and the timber may have originated from the same source but this has not been substantiated.

The Cross Keys Inn, opposite the Copper Inn, is 400 years old. Cross Keys is one of the oldest British inn names, although relatively few inns with this name survived the Dissolution of the Monasteries; it being a sign of St Peter and the Papacy. At the time of the Reformation many inn names changed to underline the allegiance of their owners, like the King's Head and the Rose and Crown. The latter is a Tudor symbol.

A story about the Cross Keys in Pangbourne, however, suggests that it got its name because the keys of the parish church of St James the Less were originally lodged at the inn and collected from there in order to open the church!

The historic Old George Hotel stands on the Square in the centre of the village. There has been an inn on this site since 1295 when the innkeepers paid a tithe to the steward of the Abbot of Reading.

In those days Pangbourne was barely a village and the only building existing then at the junction of the River Pang with the Thames was undoubtedly the first George Hotel. When the wool staplers drove their packhorses across the Berkshire Downs heading for the east coast they would certainly have stopped for refreshment there. The cellars were filled in during the year 1603 when the Berkshire witch, Betty Price, was captured there; tradition has it that she solemnly cursed the parson and all who had a hand in her arrest.

In 1783 the landlord of the George was the indomitable Tom Johnson whose horses and hounds were famous throughout the country. At the age of eighty-two he rode non-stop from Carfax in

The George Hotel in 1880

Oxford to Pangbourne. Details of this great race were solemnly reported in *The Times*.

Towards the end of the nineteenth century the George had a landing stage just upstream from Whitchurch Bridge and offered its customers boating and fishing facilities as well as livery stables. In 1923 the Old George was almost gutted by fire and was largely reconstructed in 1924. It has suffered from fire again since then and although it has now been much altered and modernized it retains some of its old character.

The Swan Hotel by the weir dates from 1642 and in the days when barges carried goods along the river part of the hotel was used as a grain store. It is perhaps best known as the inn where Jerome K. Jerome's *Three Men in a Boat* ended their journey down the Thames over a hundred years ago. Jerome, Harris, George and Montmorency the dog arrived at Pangbourne on a pouring wet evening in 1888. They were cold, dirty and very wet and leaving their boat and all it contained with the boatman at the Swan they set off for Pangbourne station and the 5 o'clock train to London with local resident, Harry Champ, carrying their luggage.

By some historical quirk of the electoral boundaries the Swan formed an island of Oxfordshire in Berkshire and up until the 1990s

The Swan Hotel, c. 1900

appeared in a separate register of electors of the Henley constituency. When Oxfordshire and Berkshire licensing hours differed the Swan had a bar in each county and it is said that customers would extend their drinking hours at closing time by moving from one bar to the other.

— 9 —

Revels and Celebrations

A century ago in many parts of England country wakes or fairs were held with sports and pastimes. They were held annually and were often connected with the feast of the dedication of the church, though probably they were adapted from much earlier pagan rites. In early times people were ordered to make booths and tents with the boughs of trees in the churchyard and there to celebrate the feast with thanksgiving and prayer and not betake themselves to drunkenness and debauchery. Very soon there were undesirable accompaniments to the thanksgiving and prayer and by degrees the religious wake became a secular fair, bearing no relation to its religious origins.

In the eighteenth century the fairs locally had become a 'revel' and the *Reading Mercury* of 8 July 1776 announced one to take place in Pangbourne:

Pangbourne Revel is to be held at William Newman's (sign of White Swan) in Pangbourne on 18/19 July 1776 starting at 3.0 pm.

Prize of gold laced hat valued at 27s. to be played for at cudgels. The man who breaks most heads wins. 2/6 to each man who breaks a head and 1/- to each man whose head is broke. Blood to run an inch to count as a break.

On second day only a Holland smock offered for a prize for a woman's race in four heats. Also bullet to be dipped for in a tub of flour, winner is one who finds it the fastest. Jackass race with prize of half a guinea.

It seems likely that the contestants in this revel would need the administrations of one James Monckton who advertised in the *Reading Mercury* in October of that year as follows:

> INNOCULATION. James Monckton, surgeon and apothecary in Pangbourne acquaints his friends and the public in general that his house will again be opened for the reception of patients under innoculation on Monday 17th October when those patients who chuse to put themselves under his care may depend on being duly attended. And a family will be waited on at their house . . .
>
> NB. Poor people within three miles of Pangbourne will be innoculated gratis.

There was a great deal to celebrate in the last ten years of the nineteenth century and the people of Pangbourne made the most of the momentous occasions.

A civic procession in the High Street, probably during the First World War

Pangbourne Revels, dancing in the Square in the 1930s

'Wing's for Victory' fête in the grounds of Pangbourne Lodge

Queen Victoria's Golden Jubilee

On Wednesday 8th July 1887 the parishioners assembled at 12.30 and, preceded by a band, marched to the church for a Special Service appointed by the Archbishop of Canterbury. At two o'clock 470 adults sat down to dinner in the large shed in Mr E.T. Ashley's boat yard, there hardly being an absentee. In the afternoon there were games and sports on Pangbourne meadow and at 5 o'clock a substantial tea for 182 children. Tea was again provided for 440 adults at 6.30 and in the evening there was a firework display. The village was well illuminated with gas jets, coloured lamps and Chinese lanterns with an abundance of flags and nothing whatever occurred to impair the harmony and pleasure of a most delightful day.

(Taken from *A Short Account of the Parish of Pangbourne* by the Revd Robert Finch)

Queen Victoria's Diamond Jubilee

On 8th July 1897 the celebrations began with the church bells ringing from 5.0 to 6.0 am and, during the morning, the 3rd Royal Berkshire Regiment played in different parts of the village before marching to church at 12.0 o'clock for a Choral Service of Thanksgiving. The Boat House, lent by Mr Webb, was transformed into a dining room bedecked with flags and flowers for the 500 guests who enjoyed a substantial dinner served by Mr Hull of The George. At the 5.0 o'clock tea, provided for the children and those unable to attend the dinner, each man was supplied with half an ounce of tobacco and every child under 15 was presented with a Jubilee medal and a mug. The number entertained at dinner and tea was not far short of 900. During the afternoon celebrations continued on Pangbourne meadow with sports, swings, a Punch and Judy Show and free trips on the steam launch 'Lottie' which afforded much enjoyment. The day ended with fireworks let off from Thames Bank, but the village was *en fete* for many hours afterwards. Most of the houses were decorated with flags and appropriate mottoes and there was a torchlight procession in which a number of bicycles and members of the Fire Brigade

took part adding much to the picturesqueness of the scene.
(From *Pangbourne Parish Magazine*, August 1897)

The Relief of Mafeking

The parishes of Pangbourne and Whitchurch decided on a joint celebration to mark the relief of Mafeking in May 1900. In fact, there were two celebrations, one on the Saturday when the news of the victory was received and another on the following Monday when it was confirmed.

Whitchurch Mill and Church, c. 1887

On the Saturday the Whitchurch Fire Brigade with their two 'manuals' joined the Pangbourne 'manual' and a procession of youths carrying flaming torches visited, first, Mr Walker's house at Tidmarsh, then Bere Court, back into Pangbourne village, up Shooters Hill round by Horseshoe Road and back through the Moors and Thames Avenue. The Pangbourne Drum and Fife Band kept matters lively with the procession joining in the patriotic songs. Finally a huge bonfire was lighted in the centre of the village and the villagers made merry until early the next morning.

The Monday procession was much more elaborate with nearly all the tradesmen's carts decorated with flags, fairy lamps and Chinese lanterns. A carpenter's shop was fitted up by Mr Boxall with two forges sent by Mr Holmes and during the journey fourteen horse shoes were satisfactorily made. After a final procession round Whitchurch, the bonfires began.

Mr Payze's bonfire burnt an effigy of President Kruger and the heat from a monster bonfire, fed with tar barrels, paraffin tubs and a load of bavins, was so intense that it scorched the paint outside the George and broke two or three windows.

The enthusiasm of the crowd was at concert pitch and it was 3 o'clock before the merry proceedings came to a close round the dying embers of the fire. The collection made for Lady Curzon's Mafeking Relief Fund reached the satisfactory sum of £24 2s. 4d. Although the report in the local press made no mention of refreshments it is said, on good authority, that at some time during the day there was a free pint of beer for each man and half a pint for the ladies.

— 10 —

Around Pangbourne

The area immediately around the village contains some interesting houses and other features that merit inclusion in a book of Pangbourne, partly because of their close proximity, but also, sometimes, because of the way that their history has related to village life over the years.

Basildon Park

Basildon Park, lies two and a half miles from Pangbourne on the road to Streatley and is now owned by the National Trust. The house has a beautiful setting overlooking the Thames, and was built between 1776 and 1783 by Sir Francis Sykes, a Yorkshireman and wealthy nabob of the East India Company. Designed by John Carr of York, it is based on a Palladian villa plan and, built in a honey coloured Bath stone, it is acknowledged to be one of his masterpieces. In 1838 Syke's grandson sold the estate to the haberdasher and Liberal MP James Morrison, for whom J.B. Papworth redecorated some of the rooms and enlarged and embellished Carr's lodges on the Streatley Road.

Between 1910 and 1952 Basildon Park was unoccupied (apart from being requisitioned by the military in both wars) and its contents and many of its fittings were dispersed. When Lady Iliffe first saw the house in 1952 it was derelict, cold and damp, but impressed by its atmosphere of former elegance and its feeling of solidity, she and her husband, rather than condemn it to almost certain demolition, decided to restore the house to its former glory. After years of

Gilbert Beale feeding birds in the wildlife park in the 1960s

Basildon Park photographed in the early years of the century

rebuilding and refurbishing, often done by Lady Iliffe herself, the house was ready for occupation and it remained the Iliffe home until 1978 when Lord Iliffe presented it, with its contents and surrounding parkland, to the National Trust. He also made a large endowment with the wish that the Trust should protect the house and its park for future generations to enjoy.

Basildon Park is open to the public in the summer season and has a fine collection of pictures, furniture, and an unusual decorative shell room.

Child-Beale Wildlife Park

About a mile and a half from the village, along the road to Streatley, is the Child-Beale Wildlife Trust Park. The park is a registered charity and was created in 1956 by the millionaire Gilbert Ernest Child-Beale who had the vision of preserving this beautiful part of the Thames Valley for public enjoyment. The site at this time consisted of little more than a small pond, a farm, dirt road and his famous peacocks, the descendants of which can still be seen roaming the park. There was also at that time a pavilion which he had designed and erected in 1956 as a memorial to his parents.

Purley Hall with the Wilder family on the lawn, c. 1884

Gilbert Beale was quite a character. As an old man he could often be seen touring the grounds in his vintage Rolls Royce to see how things were going; one day they did not go as well as he might have expected! A resident of Upper Basildon tells how one Saturday afternoon, when Gilbert Beale was ninety-four years old, he saw the old man driving his friends round the Park in his Rolls when suddenly the car swerved from the track and went straight into the river. Fortunately a number of people who were nearby rushed to the spot and the occupants were rescued without serious injury. But the rescue was not without its drama. The *Daily Mirror* of 1 October 1962 reported that for several seconds, as the car was sinking, Gilbert Beale struggled to free himself from the driving seat. Also trapped in the car were two ladies, two gentlemen and two pet dogs. Among the sightseers on the river bank were five of his employees who dived into the river, opened the car doors, and brought out Mr Beale and his friends. Seconds before the car completely submerged one of the rescuers went back for the dogs, a pug and a terrier, and rescued them too. The Rolls was restored to its former glory, but Gilbert Beale never drove it again.

When he died in 1967, at the age of ninety-nine, his great-nephew Richard Howard took over the responsibility of running the Trust and with help from his family and a dedicated staff, the Trust's development grew apace: ponds and lakes were created, ornamental statues and fountains brought in and trees planted to give the park its present character. Today the Beale Bird Park has many beautiful birds including flamingos, owls, parrots and the national collection of pheasants. Other attractions of the new park include a large children's playground, a small gauge passenger railway and daily river fishing.

Purley Hall

Purley Hall, originally Hyde Hall, stands about a mile from the village along the Reading Road and was built by the Hyde family in 1609. Edward Hyde was Charles I's Secretary of State and during the Civil War the family went to Belgium with the exiled royal family. While there Edward Hyde's daughter Anne married James, son of Charles I, who later became James II and two of their daughters became queens: Queen Mary and Queen Anne.

After the Restoration the Hyde family returned to England and

Edward became Charles II's Lord Chancellor and the first Lord Clarendon. He later fell from favour after a defeat in the wars with the Dutch and was wrongfully sent into exile where he died in poverty. It is not known whether Purley Hall was ever used as a Royal residence, but James II's coat of arms is emblazoned over the front door and, as the Royal family had strong Catholic inclinations at that time, it is possible that its secluded position was sometimes found very useful.

Edward Hyde's first wife, Anne, died at Purley Hall and is buried in Purley churchyard.

In 1720 the Hydes sold their heavily mortgaged estate to Francis Hawes, an extremely controversial figure and director of the great eighteenth-century banking swindle known as the 'South Sea Bubble'. When the investment 'Bubble' burst Francis, like thousands of others, met with financial disaster. He went bankrupt in 1723, having spent lavishly on the mansion, but he stayed on at the Hall sharing the house with his brother Thomas who bought the property for £1,080. Purley Hall remained in the possession of the Hawes family until 1770 when it was sold to John Wilder of Nunhide and Shiplake. It stayed with the Wilder family for 190 years.

In 1778 it was let to Warren Hastings, the first Governor-General of India, who lived there from 1788–94 while he was tried for alleged corruption and ill-dealings in India. It is said that he prepared his defence while at the Hall and was eventually acquitted with honour. While there he also farmed, breeding cattle and horses, and collected a large menagerie, his celebrated 'Indian Zoo', which was kept in the park.

From the turn of the century until 1961 the house was leased to a succession of families and latterly fell into some disrepair, but was greatly restored by Major and Mrs Bradley who owned it from 1961 until the early 1980s.

Today Purley Hall, is privately owned and not open to the public.

Mapledurham House

The village of Mapledurham lies to the east of Pangbourne on the Oxfordshire bank of the river and can be reached by crossing the Thames at Whitchurch Bridge to reach the B4526 (Caversham–Goring Road). Mapledurham has been the home of the Blount family, ancestors of the present owner, Mr J.J. Eyston, since 1490 when Richard Blount of Iver in Buckingham purchased part of the present parish, Mapledurham Gurney, from the Lynde family.

The village has remained unspoilt for 100 years with its church, almshouses, watermill and Manor House. The house stands in parkland which runs down to the Thames and was built about 1588 by Sir Michael Blount and later fortified for the King during the Civil War. The house was once frequently visited by the poet Alexander Pope and there are portraits in the house of the two sisters with whom he was in love. The private chapel, built in 1789 by special licence, is of great beauty and interest. In the porch of the church there is the story of the time in 1976 when the village was transformed into a film set for the shooting of sequences for the film *The Eagle Has Landed*.

The village watermill is the last working corn and grist mill on the Thames and visitors can see the mill producing wholemeal flour which can also be purchased in the mill shop. It is used by several local bakers.

The house and watermill are open to the public during the summer months.

Westbury Farm Vineyard

Just over a mile from Pangbourne along the Reading road there is a sign, on the left, to Westbury Vineyard. The vineyard was started in 1968 by Bernard Theobald as an additional farming enterprise following the realization that not only had the vine been grown successfully in England since Roman times, but that the Thames Valley had been famous for growing the best wines. Now extending over 16 acres, it is one of the largest established vineyards in the country.

The farm is an ancient holding with early British and Roman remains. The foundations of the old cow-shed are thought to date back at least 1,000 years, while the barn, which is now a lecture theatre, is Tudor as also is part of the farmhouse, the remainder being Queen Anne.

There is now also a farm shop and three trout fishing lakes. Guided tours for parties are available during the summer months.

—11—

Pangbourne Today

Pangbourne today is a busy modern village with a population of 2,583 (1981 census). Although it is busier and noisier than it was at the turn of the century it is still considered by many to be one of the most attractive villages on the River Thames and is increasingly a popular place to live. Shopping in Pangbourne has changed considerably since the days of the small trader, but the village is still well-catered for with a supermarket, a butcher, a chemist, greengrocers, ironmonger, newsagents, a launderette, hairdressers, off-licences and a variety of places to eat.

The modern village has a wide range of clubs and organizations catering for all ages, from an operatic and dramatic society and a Silver Band to sports and a variety of charity groups.

In 1982 the village was 'twinned' with Houdan in northern France and an active Twinning Association exists to arrange family and school exchanges.

Among the special facilities of the village an important one is the County River Centre at Dolphin House, donated for the youth of Berkshire by John Dolphin who lived at Whitchurch Mill. Built in the 1960s beside Whitchurch Bridge and Pangbourne Meadow, the centre is a nationally recognized facility for training young people in outdoor pursuits, particularly those related to water sports. There are courses in kayaking, canoeing, sailing and wind-surfing as well as caving and climbing.

The village sign, which was erected in 1961 by the car park in Station Road, shows King Burtulf with the charter of 844 and a Saxon ship over the name of the village. Kenneth Grahame's book and the symbolic willows add a modern touch to the design